Be sure to check out Mike Riley's other books:

Murders Unsolved: Cases That Have Baffled The Authorities For Years

"The body was wrapped in a plaid blanket, and placed inside a box that had once held a baby's bassinet purchased from J.C. Penney's. The boy was clean and dry, and recently groomed. However, he looked to be undernourished. Clumps of hair found on the body suggested he had been groomed after death."

Check it out on Amazon in the Kindle eBooks Category

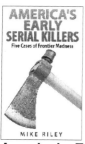

America's Early Serial Killers: Five Cases of Frontier Madness

"We tend to think of those early settlers as hard working, decent people only looking for religious freedom and better opportunities for their families. However, even during those times, people existed who were depraved, evil and mentally ill. These are some of their stories."

Check it out on Amazon in the Kindle eBooks Category

Table of Contents

Introduction

During the research phase of this book, information was gathered from university libraries, archives and the Internet. While every effort was made to verify the information contained here, it should be noted that as time goes by facts of the stories may become less clear as peoples' memories fade and witnesses pass on.

One of the most terrifying ordeals most people can imagine is for a loved one to disappear without a trace. Unfortunately, it does happen and to those who have experienced it, heartfelt and sincere sympathy goes out to you.

If many of the older stories had occurred in modern times, it's more probable the cases would have been solved. Our current forensic and analytical procedures, especially DNA analysis, add many more tools for law enforcement to use while solving cases.

Imagine how many of these cases would have had a different result if they had happened in current times. Even with all of the tools at our disposal, however, people do still disappear.

Following are stories from ancient Roman times to today. The cases all differ by victim, circumstances, timeframe, assumptions and current status. The thing they have in common, of course, is the fact that someone has gone missing and is still not found.

A Slave Becomes A Hero

Missing Person: Spartacus
Date: 71 BC
Last Known Location: Reggio Calabria, Italy

Backstory:

The legend of Spartacus is widely known, but precious little is actually known about the real man. Ancient sources state that he was a Thracian, a group of Indo-Europeans that lived across a wide area in south Eastern Europe.

Some sources list him as a soldier who had once served with the Roman army, only to then be taken as a prisoner and then sold off as a gladiator. Others say that he became enslaved after he deserted the army. Which version is correct is not known. In some accounts, his wife was also enslaved alongside him.

The historical meaning and use of the name Spartacus itself supports what is known of the man. The name has links to the Black Sea region, and was also used by Thracian kings.

Whether enslaved or captured as an army deserter, Spartacus became a famous Roman gladiator. However in 73 BC he escaped. A large group of gladiators plotted escape together, and while the overall plot was foiled, a group of around seventy warriors (including Spartacus) were able to escape by fighting with kitchen tools.

They then also defeated a small force that was sent to recapture them, and after recruiting other slaves, set up in a defendable position on Mount Vesuvius. Spartacus, along with two others, was chosen to lead the group.

On The Day In Question:

The initial response against the escapees from the Romans was less than it might have been, as the Roman legions were absent, fighting in Hispania (the Iberian Peninsula) and also the Third Mithridatic War. At the time, the escapees were also seen as more of a rebellion rather than threatening outright war, and their escape was treated less seriously.

At first, Roman militia surrounded the camp at Mount Vesuvius, thinking that Spartacus and his fellow escapees would simply starve to death and be forced to surrender. Instead, the men climbed down the cliff side on vine ropes they had made previously and killed the majority of the soldiers in the Roman camp.

A similar result happened the second time Rome tried to capture the men, and this time they nearly killed the lieutenants and also took control of their military equipment.

Word of their exploits traveled, and soon others were joining the cause. The ranks of Spartacus's army had now grown to around 70,000.

Evidence of great understanding of military tactics during these battles supports the theory that Spartacus had military training and experience. While not all the local men joining had this same experience, they had access to local materials and knowledge that helped to defeat the Roman armies.

Over the next winter, the group trained new recruits and expanded their territory. By the spring of 72 BC, the group moved from their winter camp and began to travel further north. At the same time, the Roman forces were becoming more alarmed by their success, and sent two consular legions to combat their forces.

The legion was successful at first, managing to defeat a group of 30,000 men lead by Spartacus' fellow leader

Crixus. However, their success was not to last and the legion fell against the slaves lead by Spartacus.

Further alarmed by this defeat, Rome charged a man named Marcus Licinius Crassus with ending the rebellion once and for all. Licinius was the wealthiest man in Rome, and also the only volunteer. He was given access to 40,000 Roman soldiers, who he treated harshly and with brutal discipline.

For reasons unknown today, Spartacus and his men had retreated to southern Italy. Around the same time as Crassus was marshalling his army, Spartacus began to again move northwards. It was now 71 BC. Crassus saw a chance and deployed six of his eight legions, sending his general, Mummius, with the two remaining legions to move in behind Spartacus's men.

General Mummius was ordered not to engage with the escaped slaves, but perhaps he saw an opportunity too good to pass up, and he attacked. They were initially successful, and forced Spartacus' group further south as the Roman soldiers gained the upper hand. By the end of the year, Spartacus was camped in what is now Reggio Calabria in Italy.

From here, there are reports that he tried to make a deal with pirates to transport him and approximately 2,000 of his men to Sicily. He was hoping to incite a revolt, rebuilding his armies with more men. However, the pirates did not help, instead taking the money offered and leaving the rebels stranded.

Some other sources reference attempts at building rafts by the group. However, Crassus foiled their plan. It is not known how but he was able to stop the group from being able to travel to Sicily.

Spartacus' army retreated into Reggio Calabria, and Crassus' men built fortifications behind them, cutting them off from escape and supplies and creating a siege environment. Around the same time, some of the Roman legions returned and were sent immediately to assist Crassus.

Because of this action, there was some dispute as to who would receive credit for bringing Spartacus' group down, and Spartacus himself tried to take advantage of this by attempting to create an agreement between him and Crassus. However, this attempt also failed and so a portion of his group then fled towards the mountains. Crassus' forces followed.

When the legions were successful in capturing a smaller group of the escaped slaves who were separated from the main army, discipline within their ranks broke down and they attacked the oncoming legions independent of each other.

Spartacus responded by turning his army around and took a last stand against the legions, bringing their entire strength to bear upon them, the result being that the vast majority of Spartacus' army fell on the battlefield.

Investigation:
In 71 BC a final battle took place in Senerchia, an Italian municipality. It is here that multiple accounts all claim that Spartacus died in battle, but officially his body was never found. Did he survive the battle, or simply go unidentified, laid out with thousands of dead compatriots?

Current Status:
Spartacus does not seem like the type who would turn and run if his army was facing defeat, but perhaps he thought if he retreated he could rebuild his forces and his cause could live to fight another day. After the battle, the Romans crucified over six thousand survivors. Their crosses lined

the Appian Way. Perhaps Spartacus was among them, standing to the last with his men and yet unnoticed at the very end. We will never know.

The Princes In The Tower

Missing Persons: Edward V of England and Richard of Shrewsbury
Date: 1483
Last Known Location: The Tower of London

Backstory:
Edward V of England was born in Westminster, United Kingdom in 1470. His father was Edward IV, King of England and his mother was Elizabeth Woodville, from an aristocratic English family. Edward V was the eldest of two sons of the King and Queen. Richard of Shrewsbury was three years younger. The royal couple also bore seven daughters.

In 1483, Edward IV, died with little warning, after being ill for several weeks. Edward V was only twelve years old when the king died. Overnight, he was suddenly the King of England.

On The Day In Question:
When Edward IV died on April 9th, his son Edward was in Ludlow, a town around twenty-eight miles from Shropshire, England. The dead king's brother was located in Middleham in Yorkshire, and did not hear of his brother's death until April 15th. It's reported that upon hearing the news, he publically pledged his allegiance to his nephew, the new king.

According to the Croyland Chronicle, a noteworthy (but not always accurate) source for medieval English history, the now dead Edward IV had appointed the role of Lord Protector to his own brother, named Richard. This title meant that he was, temporarily, the head of state until the young Edward V was old enough to rule in his own right.

Both Richard and young Edward started to travel towards London, and met on April 29th in a parish named Stony

Stratford. It was here that rather than supporting the young king, Richard instead arrested Edward's entire team of advisors, a group that included Edward's other uncle and a half brother. The group was taken to stay at Pontefract Castle and several months later in June, the entire group was beheaded.

After that, Richard took Edward into his own custody. The move prompted Elizabeth Woodville, Edward's mother, to take Edward's brother (also named Richard) and their sisters into sanctuary.

Edward and Richard did both arrive in London, and a coronation was planned. However it was moved from the original date of May 4th to June 25th. On May 19th, Richard moved to the Tower of London, which was traditionally where English monarchs stayed before their coronation. On June 16th, his brother Richard joined him, having until this time been in sanctuary.

It was at this time that the coronation was postponed indefinitely, and on June 22nd a sermon given at St. Paul's Cross Church claimed the elder Richard was the sole legitimate heir. A petition was raised by some of the nobility for Richard to become the new king, and both of the young princes were then deemed illegitimate by Parliament.

This was further confirmed by a later Act in 1484. It claimed that due to a pre-contract of marriage between Edward IV and Lady Eleanor Butler, the marriage between Edward and Elizabeth was invalid. However, in modern times the legitimacy of this claim is hotly debated.

Richard was crowned and became King Richard III on July 3rd, 1483.

Investigation:

After Richard took over the throne, the two boys were sighted less often as time went on. A friar from Italy visiting in the 1480's reports that the two princes had been moved further inside the tower.

At the time, Edward had a doctor visit regularly. The doctor said that Edward was acting 'like a victim prepared for sacrifice' and that Edward believed that he would soon die. There are some who believe the doctor was John Argentine, who later served as a senior advisor of Kings College in Cambridge and a doctor for Arthur, the son of King Henry VII (January 28th 1457 to April 21st 1509). However, this is in some dispute.

Shortly after Richard also arrived to stay at the tower, there were reports of them playing together on the grounds of the Tower. However after the summer of 1483 there were no further confirmed sightings. A rescue attempt was launched towards the end of July of the same year, but it failed. Neither boy was ever seen alive again.

Current Status:

Many historians over the years believe that the two boys were murdered at Richard's orders. Some believe the gruesome act had been carried out as early as August 1483, just a month after Richard's own coronation. They claim that an early rebellion in 1483 shifted support from rescuing the brothers to supporting Henry Tudor (who would eventually defeat Richard and take the throne himself) because insiders highly suspected that they boys were already dead.

Other historians believe that perhaps the princes were still alive in July 1484, when a reference from household regulations of Richard III's stated that 'the children should be together at one breakfast.' However, skeptics have claimed that there is no evidence as to who 'the children' really were. There were other children currently living in the household, including the princes' two sisters.

In 1674, workers remodeling the tower discovered a wooden box containing two small human skeletons. They were not the first skeletons of children to be found within the tower, and they were reburied under a staircase. Four years after their discovery, the bones were placed in an urn and interred at Westminster Abbey on the order of King Charles II.

Much later, in 1933, the bones were re-examined by a prominent anatomist and the president of the Dental Association. They discovered non-human bones included along with human ones, and many bones missing or damaged by the workmen. However, their examination has since been criticized for making the assumption from the start that they belonged to the boys, and only looking to determine cause of death.

We do not even know if the bones definitively belonged to a male or female. No further examination has even been undertaken, and no attempt has ever been made to extract DNA from the bones. Even if we could identify the bones as belonging to the young princes, it would not prove who or what killed them.

The bones of two children were also discovered in the vault of Edward IV and Elizabeth in 1789. However, the tomb was inscribed with the names of two other children who died before the king. The tomb was resealed. Then, in the early 1800's, two coffins clearly labeled as belonging to the same children were found under the Wolsey tomb house.

So who were the bodies already in the vault? The new coffins were moved into the tomb, but no attempt was ever made to thus identify the two bodies that had already been named as the same children. Royal consent would be needed to open and examine the bones, and as yet it has not been given.

Although for many, Richard III remains the most likely suspect in the disappearance of the two princes, there are other theories. Some believe they were killed by Henry Stafford, the second Duke of Buckingham. He was very close to Richard III, and was executed himself in November of 1483.

Stafford was himself a descendant of Edward III and may have been hoping to accede to the throne. He is the only person, aside from Richard III, to be named in an official document as being in charge of the princes' welfare. However, if he had indeed murdered the princes, why did Richard not lay the blame at Stafford's feet after he was executed?

Subscribers to this theory believe that its likely Stafford would have needed Richard's help to gain access to the boys in the tower. Thus, if he was involved it's unlikely that it was without Richard's knowledge or consent.

Another theory suggests that Henry VII, who would become king after Richard III, was the one to murder the boys. Upon claiming the throne, he did execute other rival claimants, including Richard III's illegitimate son. However, the only opportunity he would have had to kill the boys was in 1485, as he was out of the country when they initially disappeared.

However, in order to cement his claim on the throne, Henry married the princes' older sister. So that his own wife's legitimacy would not be called into question he repealed the Act that had declared the princes illegitimate originally. It's suggested that he then murdered the boys as he himself removed a major obstacle blocking young Richard's claim to the throne.

Other suspects include John Howard (first Duke of Norfolk), Margaret Beaufort (Henry VII's mother) and Jane Shore (Edward IV's mistress), however most historians do not take any of these claims seriously. The main sticking point is that just about anyone would have needed permission of Richard III to access the boys in the tower.

Others believe that Edward died of natural causes, but Richard remained alive. Contributing to the mystery, a historian named David Baldwin believes that it would be impossible for no one to know what happened to the boys, or if they were still alive. Therefore, no claim could be made either way.

If it was claimed they were dead and they were still alive, too many people would have known the truth, but neither could either Richard III or Henry VII declare them alive when the boys may well have had a stronger claim to the throne than either of them. It seems that there was nothing the two kings could do but have the boys mysteriously just vanish.

During Henry's reign, two separate people claimed to be Richard, but neither claim was ever substantiated.

In 2012, bones found buried under a Leicester car park were DNA tested, and after two years of research and hunting for descendants to test from, evidence suggest that the bones could very well be those of Richard III. The University of Leicester confirmed the identification in February 2013. Although there is now some doubt to the identification, it seems perhaps a fitting end for a king who likely murdered two young children to get his hands on the throne of England.

The Mystery of the Mary Celeste

Missing Persons: Captain Benjamin Briggs, his wife
Sarah Elizabeth, their daughter Sophia Matilda, and all
seven crewmembers of the *Mary Celeste*
Date: December 5, 1872
Last Known Location: Somewhere near the Azors
(suspected)

Backstory:
The mystery of the Mary Celeste is perhaps one of the
most well known maritime mysteries. The ship was
discovered at sea totally deserted, as if the captain and all
the crew had simply disappeared into thin air.

Built in 1861, and at first named the Amazon, Mary Celeste
was a 282-gross ton brigantine. She was originally owned
by a group of eight investors. Her first captain became ill
with pneumonia just nine days after taking command of the
ship, and died at the beginning of her maiden voyage. He
would not be the only man to die while aboard the ship.

While under her next captain, she hit a fishing boat and
had to be towed back for repairs. While at the shipyards a
fire broke out. Then, while on a trans-Atlantic crossing
under her next captain, she collided with another vessel
again.

Finally, she ran aground in 1867, and was sold as salvage
to a man from New York named Richard Haines. She was
repaired at a cost of over $8,000 (around $210,000 in
2015). She was renamed the Mary Celeste and transferred
to the American registry. The shares in her ownership were
sold to four men, including her new captain, Benjamin
Spooner Briggs.

On The Day In Question:

On December 5, 1872, the Captain of the British ship Dei Gratia, David Reed Morehouse, was concerned when one of his crew spotted a ship adrift in the choppy seas of the Azores, near Portugal in the North Atlantic Ocean.

The ship was identified as the Mary Celeste, which had left New York City seven (some sources say eight) days ahead of the Dei Gratia, and should have already arrived at her destination of Italy. After observing the ship from a distance for several hours, and then determining that there was something wrong, he changed his course to investigate and offer help.

Adding another layer to the mystery, the ship was not unknown to the captain of the Dei Gratia. In fact, before the departure of the Mary Celeste from New York, Captain Briggs of the Mary Celeste had even met with Captain Morehouse.

They had served as sailors together and were old friends. During dinner with their families, they discovered their ships had similar courses on their next voyages. However, Morehouse was still waiting for cargo when the Mary Celeste left port.

At the time the ship was found, the Atlantic Ocean was experiencing the worst weather since records had began. Hundreds of ships had been lost or abandoned. Interestingly however, the weather was fine on the day the Mary Celeste was discovered.

A boarding party was sent to the ship. They discovered that the ship's charts had been tossed about, but the crew's belongings were still present. There was enough food and water on board to last another six months. The ship's sole lifeboat was missing, and a pump had been dismantled. The ship had taken on water in the lower decks, with over three and half feet of water in the hold, but it was not sinking. However, the strangest thing they discovered was that there was not a soul on board. The Mary Celeste's captain, his family, and the entire crew had disappeared.

Apart from the captain's logbook, all the ship's papers were missing. The fore hatch and lazarette were open, but the main hatch was still sealed. Also missing was the sextant and chronometer, and the clock and compass were present but non-functioning. There were no signs of a struggle or significant damage to the ship.

The ship had begun its voyage into history on November 7th, 1872, captained by Briggs. Traveling with her husband was Sarah Briggs, and their two year-old daughter, named Sophia. The couple also had a seven year-old son, who had been left in the care of his grandmother.

Also on board were seven crewmembers. The crew's nationalities included two Americans, one Dane, and four Germans. Despite being from different countries, they all spoke fluent English. All the crew had exemplary records, and Captain Briggs had a reputation as an excellent and experienced captain, having previously captained at least five other ships and owned many more.

Ship logs indicate that they had battled heavy weather in two weeks prior to the Dei Gratia's discovery of the empty ship. The last log entry was at 5am on November 5th, 1872, and it did not detail any signs of distress.

After they discovered the ship, the crew of the Dei Gratia sailed it another eight hundred miles to Gibraltar, where it underwent a salvage hearing. Usually, such a hearing would only determine whether the salvagers (in this case the Dei Gratia crew) were entitled to a payment from the ship's insurers. However, this time the Attorney General in charge of the case suspected mischief and launched an investigation.

Investigation:

Over time, wild theories and claims have been made, including alien abduction, pirates, sea monsters, and homicidal sailors. However, through evidence since discovered and examinations by modern technology, historians now believe they know what happened to the ten people on board.

The case may have floated off into history, were it not for a published sensationalist account in 1884, by a young Arthur Conan Doyle. His article kicked off decades of speculation, and it was not until 2002 that documentarian Anne MacGregor decided to investigate the mystery and separate fact from fiction once and for all.

MacGregor had previously completed four similar investigative documentaries, including looking at the Hindenburg disaster. In each, she applied modern forensic and scientific techniques to great historical mysteries.

She first eliminated piracy, as the ship was found intact and with her full cargo still on board. Another theory held that the crew had mutinied after drinking all the alcohol (over 1,700 barrels were on board). Interviews with the crew's descendants made her also dismiss that scenario.

Another popular theory is that vapor emissions from the large amount of alcohol on board caused an explosion. Nine of the barrels were made from red oak, more porous than the rest, which were made from white oak. These nine barrels were empty. Had fumes slowly leaked out and built up in the hold? Perhaps the barrels were poorly secured, and rubbing of the metal rings caused a spark and ignited the fumes. Could an explosion, however small, have convinced an experienced captain and crew to abandon ship?

If the missing lifeboat had not been secured to the ship properly when launched, perhaps they could have been drowned or even died from exposure when left adrift. There was a frayed rope found dragging in the water.

After investigating, MacGregor does not believe an explosion was plausible. There were no reports from the boarding party of smelling fumes, and there was no scorching or other damage present on the ship.

However, a reconstruction by the University College of London in 2006 showed that it might have been possible for an explosion to be powerful enough to convince Captain Briggs to abandon ship, but leave no physical evidence behind.

Using butane and paper cubes as the barrels, the reconstruction was sealed and vapors ignited. The explosion generated blew open the hold's doors and shook the entire model, but left no scorching or signs of damage. With a relatively low flashpoint of 55.4 degrees, ethanol would not need much to ignite.

What about the homicidal sailor, suggested by Conan Doyle? MacGregor believes that the inspiration for the tale could have originated from either of two German crewmembers, brothers named Volkert and Boye Lorenzen.

They were originally believed to have been suspects as none of their personal belongings were on board. However, a descendant of the brothers reported that their things had been lost in a shipwreck earlier in 1872. MacGregor did not find any motive to support Conan Doyle's claims.

The ship was still seaworthy, and there was plenty of food and water available. The sails that had been unfurled were damaged, but the ship was in no danger of sinking. What could have convinced a Captain to take his family and crew and abandon a ship in the middle of the ocean? An experienced captain such as Briggs would not normally abandon ship unless he had no other choice.

So what did happen? Was the cause of the missing crew really an explosion, or is there a more simple explanation? MacGregor thinks there is. Notes from the initial investigation into the disappearance after the salvage by the Dei Gratia reveal that there was initially nothing unusual about the ship's voyage, but that something strange may have occurred in the last five days.

Using the transcripts, MacGregor and Phil Richardson (an oceanographer and expert in derelict vessels) plotted her course and positions over those five days. Then using data from ICOADS (International Comprehensive Ocean-Atmosphere Data Set) and other information about sea conditions of the time, they came to the conclusion that in fact the ship was actually one hundred and twenty miles further west of where they thought they were.

According to Captain Briggs's calculations, he should have sighted land three days earlier than he did. The notes also indicated that the day before they reached the Azores, Captain Briggs changed course, perhaps seeking haven.

The night of the last entry in the log, the Mary Celeste would have encountered strong winds and rough seas, but again is that enough to give an experienced captain reason enough to abandon ship?

Further research revealed that on her last voyage, the ship had carried coal, and had also recently been refitted extensively. The dust from both the coal and the refitting could have clogged and broken the ship's pumps, explaining why one was found dismantled.

Without it, Briggs had no way of knowing how much of the ship's hull was filling with water. There was simply too much cargo for him to visually measure. It may have been the final straw.

Bad weather, an unsure position, and now a broken pump with a risk the hull may fill and the ship sink, may have finally convinced Captain Briggs to abandon ship, meeting their fate aboard a lifeboat in rough seas.

Current Status:
The crew of the Dei Gratia did eventually receive a payout, but it was only one-sixth of the insured value, indicating that perhaps authorities were not entirely convinced of their innocence in the disappearance.

As for the Mary Celeste herself, another partner owner named James Winchester, sold her after his own father drowned in an incident involving the ship in Boston. The ship changed hands seventeen times in the next thirteen years.

Finally, owner G.C. Parker deliberately wrecked her in an attempt to commit insurance fraud. He was arrested and put on trial. The ship was left where she had been wrecked, and in August of 2001 her remains were allegedly rediscovered by an expedition headed by author Clive Cussler.

A Missing Child Found?

Missing Person: Robert (Bobby) Clarence Dunbar
Date: August 23rd, 1912
Last Known Location: Swayze Lake, Louisiana

Backstory:
Bobby Dunbar was born in April 1908. He was the first son born to Lessie and Percy Dunbar. The family lived in Opelousas, Louisiana. He also had a younger brother, named Alonzo.

The story surrounding the disappearance of Bobby Dunbar is not your typical missing person story. In fact, for many years it was considered solved, and the boy returned to his family. However, as in many of the cases contained in this book, sometimes things are not what they appear to be.

On The Day In Question:
Friday, August 23rd, 1912 began as a normal day for the Dunbar family. A family trip to Swayze Lake in Louisiana was planned. On the day in question, Bobby Dunbar was just four years old. While on the fishing trip at the lake, Bobby Dunbar disappeared while his family was eating lunch. It's believed that four year-old Robert simply wandered away.

Investigation:
An initial extensive search of the area surrounding Dunbar's disappearance found a set of bare footprints leading out towards a railroad trestle. A strange man had also been seen around the area, and so when the young boy was not found, authorities made the assumption that he had been abducted.

An intensive search was launched to find the young boy, but it would be eight long months before any result. In April of 1913, a man named William Cantwell Walters was discovered traveling with a young boy who matched

Dunbar's description. Walters, a traveling handyman who specialized in tuning pianos, insisted that the boy was in fact named Charles Bruce Anderson.

He claimed that the boy's mother, Julia Anderson, worked for his family and had given him custody of the boy. Despite his claims, Williams was arrested for kidnapping and the Dunbar family was contacted. They traveled to Mississippi to identify the boy.

From here, accounts differ. Some reports state that the child was immediately overjoyed when seeing his family for the first time, shouting "Mother!" and hugging his parents. Others report that the boy was wary and cried, and that Lessie Dunbar herself was unsure whether the boy was really her child.

Similar accounts were also made as to the boy's recognition (or lack thereof) of his sibling, Alonzo. The boy was later identified by his mother from scars and moles she viewed while bathing him. He was returned to the Dunbars and they took him home.

However, the celebrations were not to last long. Shortly after the boy was returned, Julia Anderson came forward, corroborating Walters' claims that the boy was in fact her child. She claimed that Walters was supposed to only have the boy for a trip over two days, but he had not returned as promised. Again, newspaper reports are unclear as to whether the boy recognized her either, or whether she could positively identify the child.

Unlike the well off and respected Dunbars however, she was presented with five different children and asked to identify which was her boy. While it may seem inconceivable for a mother to not recognize her own child, perhaps the long separation of nearly a year coupled with the great changes a young child can go through influenced her reaction.

Although she too was convinced the boy was hers, by the next day Anderson was more heavily doubted and questioned than the Dunbar family. Unlike the Dunbars, news at the time was highly critical of her supposed failure to identify him immediately. Her moral character was also called into question, including having three other children (two of whom were deceased) out of wedlock.

Her claim to the boy was dismissed, and with no money or backing to fight the decision, she returned home, leaving the boy in the care of the Dunbars. She did later return as a witness for Walters in his kidnapping trial, but she never did gain custody of the boy. Walters was released after two years without a new trial, after being granted the right to appeal.

After the trial, Anderson seemed to reinvent herself, becoming a member of the church, marrying and having seven children. Although her life was happy, she would often refer to her 'lost son' Bruce, and claim that he had been truly kidnapped in the end by the Dunbars.

The boy was raised as Bobby Dunbar, grew up, married and had four children of his own. He lived out his life as a member of the Dunbar family, and died in 1966. Everything was normal again in the Dunbar family. Until that is, somebody got curious.

Current Status:
In the years following Bobby Dunbar's death, his granddaughter Margaret Dunbar Cutright, decided to investigate the case of her grandfather's kidnapping and subsequent claims on his identity.

As well as reading media of the day and court reports, she also interviewed the children of Julia Anderson. Originally, she undertook the research to prove that her grandfather had truly been Bobby Dunbar, but as she dug deeper her own doubts began to surface instead.

Finally in 2004, Bob Dunbar Jr., Dunbar's son, consented to a DNA test. His DNA was tested against the son of Alonzo Dunbar, a man who should have been his first cousin. When the results came back, they were clear.

There was no match. Nearly 100 years after the kidnapping, the world finally knew the truth. The small boy found and fought over in 1912 was never Bobby Dunbar.

Both his true identity, and what therefore happened to the real Bobby Dunbar on that fateful day in 1912, remains unknown. Was he abducted after all? Perhaps he fell into the swamps and drowned, or was killed by an animal. We'll likely never know.

The Monster of Cinkota

Missing Person: Bela Kiss
Date: 1916
Last Known Location: Cinkota, Hungary, potentially New York City.

Backstory:
Born in Hungary in 1877, Bela Kiss was a handsome man who worked as a tinsmith. A highly intelligent man, Kiss had no formal schooling, but was a voracious reader. As well as teaching himself his trade, he could converse with even the most educated people on subjects such as literature, history and art.

He was known as a friendly and hard-working man in Cinkota, the small town near Budapest where he lived. With blond hard and startlingly blue eyes, he was considered by many to be the town's most eligible bachelor.

Despite this, he was not eager to jump into a relationship. Instead, Kiss hired an elderly housekeeper to keep his house in order, in lieu of marrying.

He kept an apartment in Budapest, and it was there he took out an advertisement in the paper looking for a companion. He began writing to women. Although many noticed a stream of young women visiting him at his home in Cinkota, no one was ever introduced to them, not even his housekeeper. They would disappear as quickly as they came.

On The Day In Question:
In July of 1916, the Detective Chief of the Budapest Police, Charles Nagy, received a phone call from a man in Cinkota. He believed that he'd discovered evidence of a murder at one of his properties. The man was Bela Kiss's landlord.

Kiss had let the lease lapse, and there were rumors that he had become a prisoner of war, or perhaps even died at the front.

Checking on the house for repairs after Kiss had left, the landlord had discovered a number of large metal drums outside the home. When one was pierced an overwhelming smell was quickly released.

A nearby chemist recognized the smell as that of human decomposition, and so the pair called the police.

Upon investigating at the home, they found the drum to contain a young woman's body. She had been strangled before being stuffed in the drum, the murder weapon still contained inside with her. Her body had been somewhat preserved by the wood alcohol inside the drum.

Investigation of the other six drums found the same gruesome contents. A young woman, strangled, stripped naked, and then stuffed inside.

Kiss's housekeeper resisted the police's attempts to investigate, shouting at them to leave her employer's belongings alone. However, once she was interviewed, she admitted that many in the village had been curious as to why Kiss had brought so many of the metal drums to his home.

There were rumors that he was storing illegal alcohol, but he had assured his housekeeper he was simply storing gasoline in anticipation of war.

Upon examination of his home and a search of the grounds, police uncovered even more bodies. Every victim, even those who had been buried, had first been preserved in alcohol and was still recognizable, and in many cases identifiable.

Aware that he was facing the biggest case of his career, the first thing that Nagy did was to inform the military that Bela Kiss was to be arrested immediately. The orders reached the army within an hour.

Investigation:
Despite the Detective Chief's quick actions, tracking Kiss would prove difficult. At the time, thousands of Hungarian soldiers were imprisoned, and the entire army itself was disorganized, its members scattered.

To make the confusion worse, both the name Bela and Kiss were very popular in the country, and there would be many men who shared the same name in the armed forces.

Upon investigating a locked room in the house, Nagy found mountains of letters between Kiss and many women. He had also kept photographs of many of them. Over time, he had offered marriage to seventy-four different women, and kept up correspondence with all of them.

It quickly became apparent to the detective that Kiss had also defrauded them, taking their entire life savings. Had he stolen their money and then murdered each one, before moving onto the next? As the investigation deepened, it appeared he had done exactly that. But where was he now?

Time passed, and nothing definitive regarding Kiss's location came to light, despite Nagy eventually finding enough evidence to prove he had defrauded and then murdered at least thirty women.

Then, on October 4th, 1916, Nagy received a message from a Serbian hospital. A man named Bela Kiss had died there of typhoid back in 1915. Another message followed, stating that he was actually still alive and currently a patient at the hospital. Nagy arrived at the hospital and was taken straight to the ward where Kiss was apparently recuperating.

However, the detective's elation would not last. He was shocked to discover that not only was the man in the bed already dead, it was not Bela Kiss. Somehow, Kiss had been warned and slipped out of the hospital, substituting the body of a dead solider in his place.

Nagy immediately made it widely known that Kiss, by now nicknamed the Monster of Cinkota, was still alive and on the run. Tips began to pour in from all over the country, sighting Kiss in more than once place at once.

Finally, in 1920 a tip came in from a member of the French Foreign Legion. A man named Hoffman had caught his suspicions, bragging how good he was with a garrote. Hoffman was also an alias that Kiss had used in the past. When the police arrived to interview him, the man named Hoffman had deserted without warning, disappearing.

Leads continued to be received. Another Hungarian solider reported that Kiss was in prison for burglary in Romania, while another reported he had died in Turkey from yellow fever.

Meanwhile, a New York City detective who had a reputation for his extraordinary memory for faces was certain that he'd seen Kiss in Times Square in 1932. This sighting lead to gossip that Kiss, by now in his sixties, was working as a janitor in New York. When police went to interview the man in question, he too had disappeared without a trace.

Current Status:
It has been noted that despite multiple alleged sightings of Kiss across the globe, no further murders were ever attributed to him, or any of the suspected aliases.

However, for a man as clever as Kiss clearly was, perhaps this means that he was simply never caught again.

The Lost Carnegie

Missing Person: Andrew Carnegie Whitfield
Date: April 17th, 1938
Last Known Location: Roosevelt Field, Long Island, New York

Backstory:
Born in 1910, Andrew Carnegie Whitfield was twenty-eight years old at the time of his disappearance. The nephew of the wealthy steel magnate, Andrew Carnegie, Whitfield graduated from Princeton University, and worked as a business executive.

As well as his job, he was an amateur pilot, and had accumulated two hundreds hours of experience. He owned a small airplane, which he occasionally flew for recreation.

On The Day In Question:
Somewhere around 9am on April 17th, 1938, Whitfield took off from Roosevelt Field, Long Island. He had plans to fly his plane from there to an airfield in Brentwood, approximately twenty-two miles away. The entire trip should have taken only fifteen minutes, but he never arrived as scheduled.

At only fifty hours short of the flying experience hours required to gain a commercial pilot's license, Whitfield was certainly experienced. His plane also had on board enough fuel to fly for over one hundred and fifty miles. Despite this, neither he nor his plane was recovered.

Curiously, on the day of his disappearance, Whitfield checked into a hotel named Garden City, located in Long Island. He used an alias, Albert C. White, and paid for the room in advance. He never checked out.

Investigation:

When police investigated the hotel room in Long Island, they found Whitfield gone but personal belongings left behind. These included his passport, engraved cufflinks, clothing, and two life insurance policies worth in excess of $6000, the equivalent of over $100,000 today.

Both policies listed Whitfield's wife, Elizabeth Halsey Whitfield, as the beneficiary. He also left behind several stocks and bond certificates that were made out to both of them.

Phone records for the room indicated that he had called his home when they had been out searching for him. An operator later recalled that she heard him say over the phone "I am going to carry out my plan."

With the sheer number of personal belongings left in the hotel room and the report from the phone operator, police concluded that Whitfield had committed suicide, deliberately ditching his plane in the Atlantic Ocean.

However, no wreckage was ever found, despite an extensive search at the time of his disappearance. Investigations also found no evidence of any stress or troubles in either Whitfield's personal or professional life.

The day after his disappearance, an employee at a hotel near Roosevelt Field reported that Whitfield, accompanied by friend Frank Steinman, cashed a check that day. Later, an officer for a cruise liner named Westerland told police that a man fitting Whitfield's description was seen boarding the ship.

There was no mention of Whitfield as a passenger, but there was a listing for Frank Steinman. When contacted onboard the ship, Steinman stated that he had not seen Whitfield for three weeks. A search on board failed to uncover any trace of Whitfield.

Neither Andrew Whitfield, nor his plane, was ever seen again.

Current Status:
After his disappearance, Whitfield's wife sued him for desertion. She has since said that she did not believe he had deliberately left her, but that she thought it the best way to bring interest and publicity to his disappearance.

Perhaps it worked, sightings of Whitfield continued to be reported for two years after he and his plane vanished that fateful day.

In 1946, Whitfield was declared legally dead, and the case is now formally closed. His case however continues to mystify people today. Was there some great unknown in his life that made Whitfield believe he could not go on? Or was there someone else involved in his disappearance, perhaps tampering with the plane?

If that were the case, why has no wreckage ever been found? Perhaps he landed elsewhere and, hiding the plane, simply walked off into oblivion. With a net worth of over $56,000 (nearly $1 million today), he definitely had the means and opportunity to simply 'disappear'.

A Real Life Dorothy?

Missing Person: Joan Gay Croft
Date: April 1947
Last Known Location: Woodward, Oklahoma

Backstory:
Joan Gay Croft was a four year old from Woodward, Oklahoma. Born October 28th, 1942, she lived with her parents Olin and Cleta and her seven year-old sister Jerri.

Her father Olin Croft was one of the wealthiest men in Woodward.

On The Day In Question:
April 9th, 1947 was a day that would go down in history in the town of Woodward, Oklahoma. On that day, a massive tornado plowed through the town. The F5 tornado (the strongest on the Fujitsa Scale) traveled on the ground for over two hundred and twenty miles at forty-six miles an hour.

It decimated everything within its path. Even today it's rated as one of the top ten most destructive tornadoes of all time. One hundred and eighty five people lost their lives, and over seven hundred others were injured.

Croft's family was one of those strongly affected by the devastation. Her mother was killed in the storm and her father critically injured. Croft herself had a large wooden splinter embedded in her leg, and her sister Jerri had other less critical injuries.

The girls were taken to Woodward hospital, and her badly injured father was transferred to a hospital in Oklahoma City.

After a frantic search by relatives, the girls were both located by an aunt. After checking on the girls, she left them in the care of hospital staff and went to volunteer at another hospital in Moreland, just ten miles away. Unbeknownst to anyone at the time, that was the last time Croft's family would see her alive.

That night, two men dressed in khaki uniforms that looked like army uniforms arrived at the hospital, and asked for Joan Croft by name. She was identified and then removed on a stretcher and placed in a waiting car.

Croft could be heard screaming that she wanted to stay with her sister, and protested against the men removing her.

However, she was a scared four year-old and so hospital staff likely did not place much credence in her pleas. Some sources report that the men were challenged by staff hearing Croft's cries. They told them they were transferring Croft to another hospital where her family was waiting.

When her aunt returned the next morning, Croft was gone.

Investigation:
Initially, investigators believed that a mistake or paperwork mix up had simply taken place, and that Croft would be found at another hospital in the area. However, the days wore on and she was not found at any of the local hospitals, or staying with any of the Croft's extended family.

Although still recovering from his own injuries, as soon as Croft's father heard she was missing he rushed back to Woodward. Along with Croft's grandfather, he posted flyers and missing person ads in many towns. Nothing ever came of it, and sadly her grandfather died shortly after from a heart attack.

For the next forty years, her father continued to search town after town, following up on any tip or rumor that crossed his path. He died in 1986, having never known what happened to his daughter.

Current Status:
All was relatively quiet on the case until in 1994, the popular NBC program *Unsolved Mysteries* ran a story on Croft's disappearance. Within two days, they had received over two hundred calls with potential leads.

One woman seemed particularly promising, sharing Croft's blood type and having a scar in the same place that Croft's leg was injured in the tornado. However, DNA tests would show that she was no relation to the Croft family.

There is also scarce information on the mystery men that night. Were they in the military, or just dressed like it to avoid suspicion? While not what some would consider wealthy, Croft's family lived very comfortably.

Is it possible that Croft was kidnapped for ransom? If so, why then did no call for ransom ever come? Perhaps Croft was more gravely injured in the tornado than originally thought, and died before the call could be placed.

Another theory is that her mother's family may have taken her, after learning that her mother had died. It seems strange that if the men were completely unrelated to the family, that they would know which hospital Joan was in and to ask for her by name.

Geraldine was Croft's half sister from her father, and so perhaps was of less interest to her mother's family. The family was questioned, but no link to Croft's disappearance could be found.

After the initial shock of the tornado died down, the bodies of three little girls remained unidentified. At first it was thought one of them must be Croft, but this was ruled out in all cases.

Others have wondered if perhaps Croft was abducted and sold in an underground adoption ring. Although there is no evidence to support this, the unfortunate reality is that such kidnappings do occur.

Did the men simply take advantage of the opportunity created by the tornado? If she ultimately survived the natural disaster and the kidnapping, it's quite possible that Croft is still alive today, somewhere in the world. She may simply have no idea who she really is.

The Ex-Husband, the Doctor or the Mob?

Missing Person: Jean Spangler
Date: October 7th, 1949
Last Known Location: Los Angeles, California

Backstory:
Jean Spangler was an American dancer and model. She was born in Seattle, and lived in Los Angeles with her mother, Florence, brother, Edward, sister in law, Sophie, and her five-year-old daughter, Christine. At the time of her disappearance, she was twenty-six years old.

Spangler had married a man named Dexter Benner, but after Christine's birth the relationship fell apart. She had married him when she was just nineteen, and divorced six months later. A long custody battle had taken place, with Spangler gaining custody in 1948, after custody had originally been given to Benner.

On The Day In Question:
As well as being a dancer and model, Spangler was also a bit part actress in films and television. On the night of October 7th, 1949, Spangler told her sister that she was going to meet her ex-husband to discuss his late payment of child support, and from there going to work on a night shoot for a movie.

She left her daughter in the care of her sister for the night and left the house somewhere around 5pm. When Spangler did not return by the following day, her sister filed a missing persons report.

Investigation:
Investigating officers found that the last person who reportedly saw Spangler alive was a clerk of a store near her home. He said that she appeared to be waiting for someone.

Curiously, when they checked on where she had gone for work, they found that her story did not check out. Although she had worked on films in the past, none of the Hollywood studios they questioned had any work in progress needing extras, or were even in session that night.

The obvious suspect in Spangler's disappearance was her ex-husband, Dexter Benner. However, when questioned he told police that he had not seen her for several weeks. His new wife, whom he had married only one month previously, told police that he had been with her at the time of Spangler's disappearance.

Two days after her disappearance, Spangler's purse was found near the entrance to Griffith Park. The straps were damaged in a manner suggesting that the bag had been ripped from her hands. Sixty police and over one hundred civilian volunteers then searched the entire park, but not a single other clue was found.

No money was found in the purse, but Spangler's sister reported she had not had any when she left that night, and therefore robbery was ruled out as a motive.

Inside the purse however, police found a note addressed to 'Kirk'. It was unfinished, and read, "Can't wait any longer. Going to see Dr. Scott. It will work best this way while mother is away." Spangler's mother was currently visiting family in Kentucky.

No one from Spangler's family recognized the names, and investigators could not locate anyone with those names tied to the case.

Interestingly, once she returned and was questioned by police, Spangler's mother remembered that someone named Kirk had picked her daughter up from the house twice. However, he had stayed in his car and she had not met him.

Spangler had also previously been involved in an abusive relationship with a man named Scotty, but according to her lawyer, she had not seen him since 1945. The man in question was an Air Corps Lieutenant, and had been involved in an affair with Spangler when she was still married to Benner. He had threatened to murder Spangler if she broke it off with him.

Nevertheless, police checked every doctor with the last name of Scott in all of Los Angeles. None of them had any patient records for someone with the name Spangler, or even Spangler's former married name.

Briefly during the investigations, the case even involved one of Hollywood's stars. At the time of her disappearance, Spangler had recently completed filming a small part in a film that starred Kirk Douglas.

Hearing about her disappearance and the note, he contacted investigators to report that he was not the Kirk in the note. He said that he knew of Spangler, but did not know her personally.

While following the Dr. Scott lead, police were told by some of Spangler's friends that she had in fact been three months pregnant at the time of her disappearance. She had talked to them about undergoing an abortion, a procedure that at the time was still illegal.

A former medical student was rumored to perform the procedure for money, but police could neither find him nor even prove he truly existed. Perhaps this was the mysterious Dr. Scott?

A link was also uncovered between Spangler and the mob. She had an association with a man named Davy Ogul, who was a known associate of Mickey Cohen, an infamous member of the Jewish Mafia who also had strong ties to the American Mafia. Ogul also disappeared just two days after Spangler's own disappearance.

To further the theory, a customs agent reported seeing Ogul and a woman matching Spangler's appearance in an El Paso hotel. Had she fled with him to avoid prosecution for something either he or both of them had done?

Ogul was already under investigation and had been indicted on conspiracy charges. When police investigated, Spangler and Ogul did not appear on the hotel register and they were not found on the premises.

Despite the Los Angeles police continuing to look for her, including distributing her photo, for several years after she went missing, Spangler has never been found. A nationwide search was launched, and a $1,000 reward offered.

Sightings were reported all over California, and also in Phoenix, Arizona, and Mexico City. None were ever substantiated and Spangler remains a missing person.

Current Status:
With so many possible leads, we may never know for sure what happened to Spangler. Was she in cahoots with the mob? One lead stated that she, Ogul, and a third man named Niccoli (who had disappeared from California) were heading for Las Vegas, but nothing ever came from the lead.

During her divorce, Spangler had claimed that her ex-husband was a cruel man. The alleged animosity did not cease once she vanished. Benner was granted custody of their daughter after Spangler's disappearance, but Spangler's mother was granted visitation rights.

Benner repeatedly prevented the visits, until he was ultimately sentenced to serve fifteen days in jail as a result.

When this happened, he took Christine and fled the state, never to return. Could such a vindictive man been mad enough to kill his ex-wife to regain custody of his daughter? It certainly seems possible.

There has been no trace of Spangler since 1949. Even after all these years, the LAPD case remains open and Spangler is still listed officially as a missing person.

Stranded on the Hollywood Freeway

Missing Person: Robin Graham
Date: November 15th, 1970
Last Known Location: On the Hollywood Freeway, California.

Backstory:
Robin Anne Graham was born on June 22nd, 1952. The daughter of Marvin and Beverly Graham, she grew up in the Silverlake-Feliz area of Los Angeles. Graduating from high school in June 1970, she attended community college and was 18 years old when she disappeared.

On The Day In Question:
The last time Graham was seen alive definitively was at approximately 2:00am on Sunday November 15th, 1970. Highway patrol officers saw her standing beside her car on the shoulder of a freeway, near the Santa Monica off ramp. Standing with her was a white male with dark hair. The officers estimated him to be in his mid twenties. He was driving his own car, a late 1950's model Chevrolet Corvette.

Graham had used an emergency call box to ask that her parents be told that her car had ran out of gas. Her parents weren't home at the time of her call, but her younger sister took the message and told her parents when they arrived home at 2:30am. Her parents immediately went to the location Graham had mentioned, but only her car was left there abandoned. Graham was gone.

Investigation:
Investigators discovered that after going out with friends, and after another friend was dropped off, Graham was dropped off at her own car at 1:45am in the parking lot of a store where she worked part time. She had then run out of gas somewhere on the freeway.

Highway patrol officers reported stopping several times to speak to Graham, but once they saw the man with her, assumed that family had come to help and did not enquire further. At first, an officer made a report that Graham had left voluntarily with the man in the Corvette.

However when questioned further he admitted that while he had seen them together he had not actually seen her departure with the man. Did he force her to go somewhere with him, or perhaps was someone else entirely involved?

Whatever happened, no further evidence was discovered and Graham's remains, if she was murdered, were never found.

Current Status:
At the time there were several other outstanding cases involving women in similar circumstances over the previous two years. These included two other young women who disappeared from cars found with flat tires.

There have also been other similar cases after Graham's disappearance, all starting from an abandoned car, often with a flat tire, and evidence in most cases that the girls had been given a ride from a man.

The other girl's bodies were eventually found, though none of their murders have ever been solved. Perhaps Graham was an opportunistic attack by a serial killer preying on young girls driving alone.

Usually, the tires of the cars showed damage but perhaps he couldn't resist her standing alone and stranded in the middle of the night.

Months after Graham's fateful day, another woman came forward and said that a man driving a Corvette had approached her after her own car stalled on a highway. The man told her he was an off duty detective and would help her, but after she refused the man drove off. While there is no proof of the incident, or any link to Graham, it cannot be dismissed outright.

The woman involved later identified the man who approached her as Bruce Davis. Davis was a former Manson Family member, a known killer, and also a suspect in the Zodiac murders. Could it be possible that Graham was another victim of the famous serial killer?

As a result of what happened in the case of Robin Graham, California highway patrol policy was changed to better ensure the safety of stranded female drivers.

Missing At The Bus Stop

Missing Person: Kevin Andrew Collins
Date: 1984
Last Known Location: San Francisco, California

Backstory:
Kevin Andrew Collins was born on January 24th, 1974. He was only ten years old when he disappeared, and his case gained national attention.

Born in San Francisco, he lived in a working class family with his parents David and Ann Collins, and eight other siblings. He attended St. Agnes School and was in the fourth grade. As well as attending school, Collins played basketball.

On The Day In Question:
Usually one of his older brothers, Gary,12, would go with Collins to basketball practice, but on February 10th, 1984, Gary was home sick.

On that day, Collins left practice early, leaving the gym somewhere between 6:10 and 6:30pm. He was seen on the corner of Oak Street and Masonic Avenue at 7:55pm, waiting at a bus stop. After that, he was never seen or heard from again. It's unknown what happened between 6:10 and 7:55pm, almost two hours.

Investigation:
In the days before Amber Alerts, national TV shows, and the Internet, the local news and print posters were the common ways of alerting the public to the disappearance of a child. The next day, posters were distributed around the area with Collin's picture, displayed on telephone poles and storefronts.

In the following days, his case was also featured on milk cartons, billboards and national magazines.

Witnesses came forward and reported that they had seen Collins talking to a man at the bus stop. He was described as being in his twenties or thirties, blond and around six feet tall. The man had a large black dog with him, possibly a Great Dane.

Another report said that Collins had been abducted by two white men and taken in a royal blue 1967 Ford Galaxy, but this has never been substantiated.

Police did have a suspect; a convicted child killer from California named Jon Dunkle. Dunkle's three known victims resemble Collins and were also of similar ages. However, no formal charges in Collins' case have ever been made.

Despite the efforts from police and multiple national reports on his case, no evidence of significance was found.

To this day, Collins remains officially missing.

Current Status:
In 1983, a made for TV movie was released about another child who went missing, Adam Walsh. Adam was six when he disappeared and was found murdered two weeks later. The popularity of Walsh's case reignited interest in other missing children's cases, including Collins'.

Warnings began to appear for parents on stranger abductions. During this time, the law enforcement response to the abduction of a child was also strengthened.

In November 2005, nearly twenty years after his disappearance, someone applied for a passport using Collins' name. However, it turned out to be only the crime of an alleged identity thief, and no link to Collins' disappearance was found.

In February of 2013, a new suspect was named in the case. Wayne Jackson used many other aliases but his physical description was similar to the blond man witnesses had reported. He lived on Masonic Avenue and was the owner of a large black dog. His now known criminal history and use of aliases finally caught up with him in 2013.

Jackson had originally been interviewed and his house searched in connection with the case in 1984, as police had known he had a conviction from 1981 in connection with the molestation and kidnapping of a seven year-old boy from San Francisco.

However, at the time of Collins' disappearance, they did not know that he also had been arrested for molesting two Canadian boys in 1973. He had jumped bail and hidden in the USA using one of his aliases.

After cadaver dogs indicated possible remains underneath Jackson's previous residence on Masonic Avenue, the concrete floor was removed. The preliminary report however indicated that the remains were of an animal. Jackson died in San Francisco in 2008 and was never formally charged in the disappearance of Kevin Collins.

An aged enhanced composite of Collins was released in 2013. He would have been 39 years old.

The Springfield Three

Missing Persons: Suzie Streeter, Stacy McCall and Sherrill Levitt
Date: June 1992
Last Known Location: Springfield, Missouri

Backstory:

The story of the Springfield Three began with a celebration. The day before, Suzie Streeter, 19, and Stacy McCall, 18, had celebrated their graduation from high school. They had plans to go on a road trip to a water park in Branson, Missouri.

On The Day In Question:

That night, the two girls had gone to a graduation party, and had planned to stay overnight with friends. However, as it turns out, a large group of out of town relatives turned up and there was no room for the girls to stay after all. They decided to return to Streeter's mother's home, arriving at 2:15am on June 7th.

That night, Streeter's mother, Sherrill Levitt, 47, had also been up late. Levitt was a hair stylist who had moved into the home after separating from Streeter's father. Levitt had been repainting a chest of drawers and spoke to a friend on the phone at 11:15pm. However, it's not known if she was still awake when the girls returned to the home.

At 9:00am the next morning a family friend, Janelle Kirby, arrived at the house along with her boyfriend. They had planned to travel with the two girls to the water park. However, they found no sign of any of the three women.

The boyfriend noticed that the porch light was broken, and while they waited for the women to return, he cleaned up the broken glass and fixed the light. Kirby would also later report that the family dog was acting in a distressed manner, which was unusual.

She also reported answering a prank call full of sexual innuendo while at the residence, but at the time did not think anything of it beyond it being an annoying joke.

Eventually they decided that Levitt, Streeter, and McCall must have gone ahead without them and they continued on themselves. There was no indication that the three women had been to the park.

Meanwhile, Levitt's home had another visitor. McCall's mother, frustrated by the lack of notice of her daughter's change in plans, stopped by the house. After nearly a full day of wondering where her daughter had gone, she had visited the house to try to find her.

She found all items of clothing McCall had taken with her still in the house, except for her underwear. The remaining clothing was all neatly folded and placed on the floor. The three women's handbags were also neatly lined up.

McCall's mother called the police. Within twenty-four hours, she had also made up her own missing persons posters, using photos from the graduation, and distributed them around the neighborhood.

Investigation:
When Levitt's home was searched, they did not find anything of significance stolen. All three women's personal items were still present, including cell phones, credit cards and handbags. If they were leaving the house voluntarily, surely those items would have been taken.

Likewise, if the motive had been robbery, it's likely that credit cards and cell phones would have been taken by whoever broke in.

None of the neighbors reported hearing or seeing anything suspicious when questioned by police. As the case officially became a missing persons investigation, over five thousand calls were made to police. However, none of them revealed anything significant.

Police also searched hills and mountains near the home, but found nothing. The boyfriend had replaced the broken porch light. The broken porch light in itself was not enough to point to foul play.

As time passed, more resources were allocated to the case, and the FBI also became involved. Levitt's eldest child, a man named Bart Streeter, was questioned but ruled out as a suspect after his alibi was confirmed.

There were other suspects, including an ex-boyfriend of Streeter's, Dustin Reckler. Reckler and his friends were known to local law enforcement and had been arrested for vandalism in the past.

The relationship with Streeter had ended some month's prior, but there was still animosity between the couple, due mostly to Streeter providing a statement to police regarding Reckler and a close associate of his, Michael Clay.

Clay in particular had been heard saying he wished death upon the missing women. The group all provided alibis of being at a local rock concert, but they were unable to be confirmed or denied.

Reckler and Clay both reportedly co-operated fully with the investigation, but have never been ruled out formally as suspects. However, neither have they ever been charged with any involvement in the disappearance.

Another witness eventually came forward at a later date, saying they had not seen the missing person posters and therefore had not made the connection initially. She claimed she saw a woman she believed to be Streeter sitting on her front porch the morning of her disappearance. The woman appeared to be in distress, and a van then pulled into the street and turned around.

The witness claims that she heard a man's voice in the back of the van telling the driver to back out slowly and get them out of there. Once the tip was released, more claims of a similar nature flooded in.

Unfortunately, the van was described in nearly every color of the rainbow and nothing ever came of the tip, despite it being mentioned multiple times in the news and detectives checking out thousands of vans.

There was one final significant suspect in the case, a man named Robert Cox. Cox was a trained Army Ranger, and had been arrested in Florida for the murder of a woman, Sharon Zellers.

The case had gone to trial, but his conviction had been overturned due to insufficient evidence. When police investigated, they found that Cox had in fact managed to evade conviction on a whole host of criminal offences, including kidnapping and burglary.

After being released from death row in Florida when his conviction for Zellers' murder was overturned, he had returned back to California to finish serving a sentence for another crime. Once released from the California prison, he moved in with his parents in Springfield. Investigators discovered that he had also worked at a car dealership where McCall's father worked as a salesman. However, Cox provided an alibi that his girlfriend confirmed, and that was the end of that.

It was not until three years later in 1995 that more evidence came to light. Then, investigators were re-examining Cox's file after he was arrested for aggravated burglary in a new case. They found the reference to Cox's alibi in the Springfield Three case.

Cox claimed that he had been with his girlfriend at church, however she had since recanted her corroboration and told police that Cox had instructed her on what to say to police.

Cox is now serving a life sentence for an unrelated case, and continues to deny any involvement in the disappearance of the three women. He does however often taunt those involved in the case with cryptic statements, such as saying he 'knows they are dead'.

Current Status:
Interestingly, it was discovered that the same day of the three women's disappearance, a concrete foundation was being poured at a hospital nearby. It would have perhaps been an ideal place to dispose of three bodies, but there is no evidence to support any such claim. It's rumored that ground-penetrating radar discovered three anomalies in the set concrete, but it has never been dug up.

While police say the case is officially still open, no arrests have ever been made. Police say that they have a list of suspects, but not enough evidence to bring any charges.

Words and Music

Missing Person: Richey Edwards
Date: February 1st, 1995
Last Known Location: Embassy Hotel, London, England.

Backstory:
Richey Edwards was born on December 22nd, 1967 and grew up in Blackwood in Wales, along with his younger sister Rachel. As a young man, he attended a university and graduated with a degree in political history.

Originally a roadie and driver for a band, Manic Street Preachers, it didn't take long for him to join the band as an official member. He did not have great musical talent, and in fact was often miming guitar playing in the band's early performances.

Instead, his contribution came in his words and design. On one of the band's albums, Edwards is credited with writing over eighty percent of the lyrics.

Edwards sometimes found himself at odds with journalists over the band's authenticity and values. After being questioned by one journalist, he carved the phrase '4 real' into his own arm with a knife.

He is said to have suffered depression severely during his life and committed other acts of self-harm. He also struggled with alcoholism and an eating disorder. Eventually, he was hospitalized for some time in a psychiatric hospital.

On The Day In Question:
On February 1st, 1995, Edwards was due to fly with fellow band member James Dean Bradfield to the USA for a promotional tour. Interestingly, in the two weeks prior, Edwards had withdrawn £200 every day from his bank account. He would have amassed £2,800 on the day of his

departure. Allegedly he had told his mother that he was not looking forward to the trip.

At 7:00am on February 1st, Edwards checked out of his hotel, the Embassy Hotel in London, and then disappeared. It is known that he drove from the hotel to his home in Cardiff, dropped off some belongings, and then left again. After that, no one has any firm evidence as to his whereabouts.

Investigation:
Investigators discovered Edwards' car parked at a service station on the 17th of February, after it was reported as abandoned. It had received a parking ticket on February 14th. The car's battery was flat, and there was evidence found to suggest that someone had been living in it.

The service station was close to a bridge, the Severn Bridge, a notorious suicide spot. From this, many people believe that Edwards, plagued by depression, chose to take his own life that day. However, he had stated previously that despite his illness, he had never been one to contemplate suicide. He saw himself as stronger than that and able '...to take pain'.

There have been other sightings of Edwards over time, such as a hippie market in India and on islands Fuerteventura and Lanzarote, both in the Atlantic Ocean off the coast of Africa. However none of these sightings have ever been substantiated or have led to further evidence.

To this day, we have no further evidence as to what happened to Edwards after he left his home that day. Did he kill himself? Perhaps public pressure and burgeoning fame became too much for his mental illness and he went into hiding. Or perhaps he met with foul play. With so little to go on, it's likely we will never know what truly happened.

Current Status:

The investigation into Edwards' disappearance itself has been criticized. A British journalist who wrote a book about Manic Street Preachers accused police of not taking Edwards' mental health into proper consideration when investigating his disappearance.

Edwards' sister has also allegedly been critical of the handling of CCTV evidence that was not analyzed until two years after his disappearance.

In 2002 Edwards' family had the option to legally declare him dead, but they chose not to. Finally in November 2008 his status was changed from missing, to presumed dead.

Taken From the Ship

Missing Person: Amy Lynn Bradley
Date: March 1998
Last Known Location: Onboard the Rhapsody of the Seas, docking in the Caribbean

Backstory:
Amy Lynn Bradley was born on May 12th, 1974 in Petersburg, Virginia. She had been awarded a full basketball scholarship at Longwood University in Virginia, and had graduated with a degree in physical education. As well as basketball, she enjoyed other hobbies such as bass fishing, pool, and playing other sports.

Bradley had just moved into a new home a month earlier, and was due to start a second job working part time with her aunt and uncle in their business. She had adopted a bulldog, and was picking her up after her return from a cruise, a vacation she was taking along with her family.

While on the cruise she had sent postcards to friends, and bought gifts to bring home. She'd also scheduled a booking for swimming lessons with a family she'd met on board. It was clear that Bradley had a life full of plans waiting for her when she returned from her vacation.

On The Day In Question:
It's known that at sometime in the early hours of the morning on March 24th, 1998, Bradley left her cabin holding her cigarettes and a lighter. She was not wearing any shoes, perhaps a sign that she did not intend to travel far or be gone for very long. It's unclear if Bradley was simply slipping out to indulge in a cigarette or she was meeting someone else.

Later in the morning of March 24th, Bradley's parents became concerned when they couldn't locate their daughter. They asked the purser's desk to back up from port and secure the ship so that no one could board or leave, but this request was denied. The purser's desk did make an announcement for Bradley to please contact the desk.

Amy Bradley was now officially missing.

Investigation:
Initial investigations discovered that Bradley's brother, also traveling with her, had left his sister sitting on an outdoor balcony and gone back to his own cabin at 5:30am on March 24th.

Other cruise passengers then reported seeing her a short time later, in the company of a man, Alister Douglas, a member of the ship's band, Blue Orchid. According to Bradley's family, she had also attracted unwanted attention from other crewmembers on the ship, some wanting to take her out for dinner.

Shortly after Bradley disappeared, the ship finished its docking procedures, and the ship was therefore accessible for anyone to board or leave.

Later that day, the Captain reported to Bradley's family that the ship had been searched completely, however her family do not believe that it was as thorough a search as management reported.

They also allege that the Captain refused to make a formal announcement about Bradley's disappearance, or post photos of her asking for more information. They say that he was concerned it would alarm other passengers.

The FBI became involved in the investigation, and they boarded the ship in St. Thomas. The FBI undertook an extensive investigation into Bradley's background. They interviewed friends, co-workers, family, employees, and basketball coaches.

They also polygraphed Bradley's entire family. It's reported that their investigation may have been somewhat hampered because Bradley disappeared outside of the USA.

In the years since her disappearance, Bradley's family have appeared on national television appealing for information, traveled multiple times to where she disappeared, and have also hired private investigators.

Her story has also appeared on the show *Unsolved Mysteries*. Although this has generated many tips, none have ever lead to Bradley's location.

One of the most promising leads was a call in response to the *Unsolved Mysteries* broadcast. A man, David Carmichael reported seeing a woman walking on the beach in Curacao with two other men in 1998.

He identified her as Bradley based on two tattoos the woman had. He claimed that he had been very close to the woman, and she made eye contact with him for several seconds, but did not speak. She was then 'whisked away' by the other two men.

A US Navy officer also reports being approached by a woman in a brothel with another woman. The woman begged him for help and said her name was Amy Bradley. He was not aware she was a missing person at the time. When he told the woman that there was a Navy ship just down the road she could go to for help, she told him she could not leave.

Worried about his superiors knowing where he was, and not realizing whom the woman allegedly was, he left without acting any further on the woman's claims.

Current Status:

Along with other leads, these two statements have led some to believe that the most likely explanation for Bradley's disappearance was that she was taken into a sex trafficking ring.

Government reports into sex trafficking indicate that around 80% of all forced prostitutes are foreigners, and that the Netherland Antilles, where the ship was docked at the time of Bradley's disappearance, is a transit and destination port for these victims.

It is now thirteen years since Amy disappeared, and there have been no further leads on her possible location since a potential identification of her in a department store in Barbados in 2005.

There is currently a $250,000 reward for information leading to her safe return and a $50,000 reward for information leading to her verifiable location.

Opportunities Missed

Missing Person: Iraena Asher
Date: October 11th, 2004
Last Known Location: Piha Beach, Auckland, New Zealand.

Backstory:
Iraena Te Rama Awhina Asher was born on July 17th, 1979. From New Zealand, she was a trainee teacher and model. She lived in Auckland.

Asher was studying for a Bachelor of Education degree as a full time student. She had been in a long-term stable relationship with her boyfriend, Julian Dyson, and by accounts from friends and family was happy and stable.

On The Day In Question:
On Monday October 11th, 2004, Asher called police on the New Zealand emergency services number. She gave her location as Piha, a beach in West Auckland, and said she was scared for her safety, and that she felt pressured for sex.

Rather than attend themselves, police decided to dispatch a taxi to the location to pick Asher up. However, the taxi went to the wrong street and ended up on the other side of the city from the beach. The taxi driver never found Asher.

Sometime later, Asher was found wandering the streets by a local couple, Julia Woodhouse and Bobbie Carroll. Ms. Woodhouse's son, Henry Woodhouse, was also present at the couple's home.

The pair took her back to their home, where she stayed for several hours. It's reported that she left their home at 1:10am perhaps feeling pressured by the close proximity of Henry Woodhouse, a single man around her age.

Later she was seen by others walking toward the beach only semi-dressed. She ran away before anyone could approach her.

That was the last known sighting of Iraena Asher. She was never seen again.

Investigation:
Asher's family told investigators that she suffered from bipolar disorder, and had run away from home in the past during an episode. During that time, her father followed her at a distance, making sure she stayed safe until she was approachable.

He had visited his daughter the day before her disappearance, and did not notice anything untoward. Asher seemed happy and stable, and was planning a barbeque for that evening.

The couple that took Asher into their home after they found her wandering told investigators that they were afraid she would bolt if they tried to call police themselves. They reported Asher's behavior as 'out of it' and told them that she said she had been given acid and ecstasy.

She told Henry Woodhouse that someone had taken photos of her on their cellphone without her permission. The couple decided to let her sleep at their house overnight, and hoped that she would be more coherent and let them call the police in the morning.

Mr. Woodhouse reports that he noticed her leaving the home in the middle of the night and attempted to stop her, but was unsuccessful.

The last people to see Asher alive were couple Zachary Nixon and Simone Ross. They were taking a late night walk with their dog. Realizing that Asher was mostly naked, they watched her for a while while hidden, and then Mr. Nixon followed her at a distance.

He followed her down an unlit track, but reports that his dog broke away from him and ran off. When he recovered the dog, he and his partner walked along the beach for several minutes with a flashlight, looking for Ms. Asher. When they failed to find her, they returned home.

They said that the woman did not seem to be in distress and they were not concerned for her. Ms. Ross said that it was relatively common for people to swim naked at Piha beach, and so they were therefore not surprised to see her in such a state of undress.

A half hour later, back at their home, the couple heard helicopters circling overhead. Looking back, they realize that this was the start of the search for Asher. A land search continued for five days, and a daily sweep of the coastline with an aerial search continued for another week. She was never found.

Current Status:
In 2012 a Coroner's Inquest was held into the disappearance and suspected death of Ms. Asher. After two days worth of evidence, the inquest ruled that she was dead, presumed drowned, and that her death was accidental.

The inquest discovered that two weeks before she disappeared, she had broken up with her long-term boyfriend, claiming a relationship with another man. She had also apparently consumed both alcohol and marijuana on the day she disappeared.

The coroner did not believe she had taken any hard drugs, as Asher had told the Woodhouse family. People who saw her during that day reported that she had seemed a little 'off'.

The coroner ruled that police contributed to her death by sending a taxi rather than a patrol car. He also ruled that the Woodhouse family also contributed to her death by not calling police. However the Woodhouse ruling was later quashed by the High Court, stating that it was unreasonable.

They found that the ruling breached the Coroner's Act and natural justice, because the couple was given no notice that their actions would be criticized, nor were they given a chance to respond to the comments.

It is not known if Asher wandered into the ocean to intentionally take her own life, perhaps suffering from an episode of her mental illness, or if she really did drown accidently. There was no evidence of her being abducted from the beach, or any physical harm coming to her on land. It is possible that her body was swept out to sea, never to be seen again.

The Road Trip to Nowhere

Missing Persons: Lyle and Marie McCann
Date: July 2010
Last Known Location: Alberta, Canada

Backstory:

Lyle Thomas McCann, 78, and Marie McCann, 77, were a married couple who lived in St. Albert, Alberta, Canada. They had three children, and were married for fifty-eight years.

In July 2010 the couple were on a road trip, traveling from their home in St. Albert to Chilliwack in British Columbia.

On The Day In Question:

On July 3rd, 2010, the McCanns left their home to start their road trip. They were supposed to pick up their daughter, Trudy Holder, at the Abbotsford International Airport in British Columbia on July 10th.

The couple was seen on July 3rd, refueling their motor home and with their Hyundai Tucson in tow. It's believed that they traveled to the Yellowhead Highway, a major highway connecting the four western Canadian provinces.

When the McCanns' failed to pick up their daughter at the airport, Holder notified the Royal Canadian Mounted Police (RCMP), and a missing persons report was filed.

Investigation:

When the RCMP released the missing persons notification, they made the connection between the missing couple and a burnt out motor home that had been discovered several days earlier.

During the evening of July 5th, firefighters in Alberta had responded to a call about a motor home on fire at the Minnow Lake campground. No bodies were found in the fire, but it was discovered that the motor home was the one belonging to the McCanns. Their car was missing.

On making the connection between the two crimes, aerial and ground searches were launched. After several days, the RCMP found the Hyundai on July 16th. It had been left near Highway 16, about 18 miles from where the burnt out motor home was found.

An announcement was then made that they believed that the McCanns had met with foul play, and the RCMP also announced a person of interest in the case.

Travis Edward Vader was thirty-eight years old and had no fixed address. There were multiple outstanding warrants for Vader's arrest, and he had a criminal history for such crimes as vehicular theft, driving a car while unauthorized, and weapons charges. He had also previously been convicted of both stealing and burning a truck.

Vader was arrested on unrelated charges. His sister revealed to the media that her brother had been staying with family in Edmonton the day after the McCanns disappeared, and that he had appeared very tired and sick.

The RCMP searched a property that belonged to an acquaintance of Vader, including searching a pond and septic tank, but nothing was found. However Vader was not released from custody.

The RCMP again searched a property in Alberta on June 27th, 2011, but the McCanns were not found.

Current Status:
On July 27th, 2011 the McCanns were declared officially deceased. The RCMP believes that the couple was killed on the day they disappeared. Vader was still in jail, having been denied bail multiple times. On April 23rd, 2012 he was charged with two counts of first-degree murder, though

these charges were stayed by the Crown on March 13th, 2014.

In February 2014, nearly four years after the McCann's disappearance, Vader launched a lawsuit against the RCMP, saying that he was being unjustly kept in custody until such time they could charge him in the McCann case.

By October of the same year he was found not guilty of nine other unrelated charges and he was released from custody. However, he was not to be free for long. On December 19th, 2014 Vader was re-arrested in St. Albert in relation to the McCann's murders.

The location of the McCanns, or their bodies, still remains unknown.

Conclusion

The National Institute of Justice has developed a resource for law enforcement, coroners, and the general public. NamUS stands for National Missing and Unidentified Persons System. It can be found online at www.namus.gov. The system consists of three separate databases.

The Missing Persons Database contains information, as the name suggests, on people who are currently missing. Anyone can enter information about a missing person. The site also provides tools for printing missing person posters.

The Unidentified Persons Database contains information about remains that have been found but not yet identified. Anyone who is interested can search the database by entering information such as age, sex, description and identifying characteristics.

The third database is the Unclaimed Persons Database. It holds information about remains that have been identified but have not been claimed by next of kin. Again, this database can be searched by name and date of birth.

All three databases are crosschecked whenever a new case is entered to aid in potential identification of the victim.

The stories in this book only skim the surface of the total number of missing persons cases. Whether a person decides to drop out of society and disappear purposely, or they meet a heinous fate at the hands of another, or nature takes its course and they are simply in the wrong place at the wrong time, the end result is that they are missing.

There is always hope that the ending of their story will become known, happy or tragic. For those left behind to wonder and worry, the waiting is the most torturous part to endure.

Dear Readers,

Thank you for purchasing this book. I enjoyed researching and writing about these cases and I hope you found them to be both interesting and engrossing.

If your friends and family would enjoy reading about this topic, please be sure to let them know about this book.

Again, thank you for your support and I look forward to writing more books of Persons Lost and Missing.

Regards,

Mike Riley

Be sure to check out Mike Riley's other books:

Hollywood Murders and Scandals: Tinsel Town After Dark

"In the late afternoon, her friends recalled, Monroe began to act strangely seeming to be heavily under the influence. She made statements to friend Peter Lawford that he should tell the President goodbye and tell himself goodbye."

Check it out on Amazon in the Kindle eBooks Category

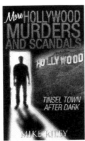

More Hollywood Murders and Scandals: Tinsel Town After Dark

"At some point in the night Reeves and Lemmon began to argue. As Reeves headed upstairs to his bedroom, Lemmon would later tell officers that she shouted out that he would probably shoot himself."

Check it out on Amazon in the Kindle eBooks Category

Printed in Great Britain
by Amazon

44740137R00043